THE
TUG OF WAR
OVER LEVERAGE

WHY SUPPLIERS LOSE

MIKE HOGENMILLER

CONTENTS

PROLOGUE

During my 42-plus-year career in retail - which included 25 years as a merchant responsible for managing relationships between buyers and suppliers - I was always amazed by the inconsistency of how suppliers defined and articulated their own self-worth.

Their lack of patience for spending the necessary time to define, validate, and communicate their company's goals, and then the path to execution, has reared its ugly head and determined the fate of some very good companies more than a few times. After I retired in 2016 and became an industry consultant, it was even more apparent as I witnessed this interesting phenomenon first-hand.

Fortunately, this self-defeating behavior can change once suppliers realize that regardless of their business, they have a multitude of opportunities available for them to:

- Substantially Improve their Position in the Market

- Gain Support and Improve Productivity while Gaining Confidence from their Associates

- Drive New Revenue with Increased Profitability

- Drive Leverage in their Favor Improving the Position with their Customers

Based on numerous conversations with suppliers and service providers, it's obvious they place more emphasis on the day-to-day and month-to-month success (or lack thereof), than they do on long-term planning accompanied by short- and long-term goals everyone involved can actually understand. When working with suppliers, the common complaints many of their associates express include:

- "It's a constant fire drill every day with something new popping up we didn't plan for."
- "I'm not sure what we are trying to accomplish other than selling something."
- "I can't seem to get the attention of my customers."
- "We are receiving customer complaints that are being answered but not solved."

All of the above are warning signs that a supplier's organization lacks effective internal planning and communication skills and if they are successful, it's most likely in spite of themselves. In just about every case like this, the success is short-lived, and the bumps in the road become sinkholes to disaster.

The book is dedicated to influencing a supplier's leadership to slow down and define and communicate their company's goals and values -- both internally and externally -- in painful detail, *including accountability and responsibility for maintaining the process moving forward*. Not just for next week or next month, but for the next three- to- five years, focusing on planning not only for the obvious opportunities I consider the *"what is,"* but also for the *"what if's,"* which are equally, if not *more* important to a company's survival and success.

Companies have to recognize that either the supplier or the buyer/customer owns the leverage. Leverage being defined as *"the dependency on someone or something to be successful in the market that they can't find anywhere else,"* leverage determines who owns the majority of the benefit and the level of success that is attainable. Guess how many suppliers don't own the leverage in the relationship with a buyer, especially with the big box retailers? Until an organization truly understands the value of what it offers the market and aligns it closely with its customer base by articulating it clearly and consistently, any potential leverage remains a distant, unrealized opportunity. The end result is a singular strategy of "just say yes" to whatever a buyer requests to avoid losing the business. Translated into practical terms, this strategy is *"the highway to an eventual dead end."*

CHAPTER 1

"I CAN'T GET A FOOT IN THE DOOR."

The most misused statement I heard multiple times from a supplier over the course of my career was:

"I can't get the buyer's attention in order for me to sell them the product they need. It's the buyer's fault we aren't successful in selling our products through their outlets."

The internal translation for the supplier should be:

"I have no idea what our competitive advantage is in the market, nor what we offer the buyer they can't do without." The key phrase here is, "can't do without."

I have a quote for the suppliers who use this as an excuse:

"If the house isn't selling, don't blame the buyers. Take the time to look at the house from the street instead of the living room and the issues will become apparent."

When we don't understand the potential for leverage that all levels of the organization could understand and support, we tend to place blame on others for our lack of success. New companies that have found niches in the marketplace are the most susceptible to short-term success leading to long-term failure. The primary cause? Their tendency to always smell the roses while failing to notice and address the thorns that ultimately show up when the roses stop blooming. This speaks to the *"What is" vs. the "What if"* scenario and identifying and planning for both in detail. With the proper planning and socialization, this is one of the key tools that will help clarify where the leverage lies in the relationship, and how to manage it going forward to your benefit.

"What is": refers to the obvious parameters that every company plans for on a regular basis. These include growth fueled by the existing market conditions that require no changes to the organization; ongoing expenses; payroll planning; raw material planning, recurring annual expenditures, etc.

"What if": refers to the not-so-obvious scenarios that occur and impact the business beyond the scope of what a company has originally planned for. The "what ifs" are usually not found in any of the planning and therefore cannot be manipulated to become an advantage instead of a demise. The impacts of "what if's" include, but are not limited to:

- Competitive consolidation
- New innovation
- New markets that have yet to develop
- Loss of an important customer
- International expansion or encroachment
- Gain of an unexpected new customer
- Sudden changes in the economic environment
- Sudden changes in the cost of doing business

I've witnessed the impact of each of these events on suppliers. When they properly planned for them, many achieved success; however, when they failed to plan for the "unexpected," it resulted in their demise.

It's all about creating and planning for change *you control* -- not managing change created by others where your company becomes the follower instead of the leader. This is a chronic issue many suppliers face today: all the control lies with the buyer or the market that creates unplanned change or no change at all. Either outcome can be problematic, with a variety of negative results.

Until you as a supplier spend the necessary time to answer the important questions, develop a plan to meet the needs that have been identified, and document the leverage and dependency you plan to enable and drive success in the market, you aren't ready to have the first conversation with a prospective buyer, much less one you currently do business with.

CHAPTER 2

THE 5 CRITICAL QUESTIONS A SUPPLIER HAS TO ANSWER

Answering the tough questions regarding how you align with your customers (the buying community), must be the initial -- and most time-consuming undertaking for the organization. The responses to several critical questions will identify the leverage points the supplier either already owns or has opportunities to own, which ultimately defines their self-worth to the market. Although the end user/consumer is important, it's a given for this book that the supplier has already developed their target niche, whether it be products or services. This isn't about what's being sold in the market; it's about how it's defined and presented to the buying community which, for our purposes, is the customer. Unless the supplier is fully integrated from manufacturing to distribution, to the final consumer acquisition, their first priority is to develop relationships with buyers who are interested in adding their products or services to their assortments, ultimately making them available to the end consumer.

Question #1: "How does your existing or targeted customer distribute/acquire product today, how many channels are they maintaining, are you aligned with both their long- and short-term strategies?"

A critical question which drives expense on both sides of the equation is the cost of distribution and transportation, which forms the initial leg of the relationship. For example, if your customer has brick and mortar locations as well as an e-commerce platform, how does your distribution now and over the long term align with theirs?

- Are they moving product through centralized distribution they own or are they fully dependent on the suppliers?
- Who owns the transportation from the factory to the final destinations: you as the supplier, the customer as the buyer, or do you share it?
- Are they buying in full truckloads or in less than truckloads and does it change by item and category?
- Are they in mechanized distribution or pallet pass through replenishment?
- Are they ordering in single store orders or in blanket orders for the total chain and redistributing at another point in their own supply chain?
- Are they doing their own e-commerce distribution, or do they depend on the supplier to do piece-pick shipping to the end consumer including last-mile distribution? Is e-commerce shared or non-shared distribution?

- What exactly are the preferred methods your buyers/customers want to use now, and in the future, and how much do they differ from yours?

- What competitive advantages or disadvantages does your distribution create for your customers?

- What are the 12- to- 18-month goals versus the 3- to- 5 year goals for you and your customer? Are they measurable, fluid, and visited on a regular basis?

Every single point in the distribution model represents a cost to either the supplier or the buyer and what is listed above isn't all inclusive. How can you present a cost of goods by item to a buyer when most of these questions haven't been answered? Many suppliers are forcing their existing, (and in many cases single method), of distribution on their buyers and assuming they will adapt to it.

This is a common problem that surfaced due to the rapid change in customer acquisition methods that has occurred over the last 20 years and continues to evolve today. We have to recognize the final end-user consumer now controls what they buy, how they buy it, who they buy it from, how it's delivered, when it's delivered, and even what they pay, due to the transparency of online pricing. If you haven't adopted a strategy to respond to the multitude of distribution platforms a buyer now requires, then you are already significantly de-leveraged in the market. Going forward, changing means aligning yourself to a greater degree with your customer and getting ahead of the curve, (rather than behind it), regarding changes in acquisition. Amazon wins big from this single point of differentiation which others are struggling to catch up with. They also continue to spend and innovate in this space; it's a large piece of the leverage Amazon currently owns. ***If the supplier is creating an advantage in distribution and transportation, the supplier improves their leverage in the relationship.***

Question #2: "Are you adequately supporting product development for both the brick- and-mortar and e-commerce channels? Is it commensurate with the actual growth occurring in each? Are your customers/buyers asking for new product or are you delivering the need before the market requests it?"

Each of these two channels is expanding in the market at drastically different rates depending on the category, (for the purpose of this book, we'll use the home improvement industry as the basis of discussion). There are a number of questions that have to be explored.

- **At what rate are your customers growing in each of these channels? Are you growing at a similar rate or something different and why?** Keep in mind, depending on the customer, most are growing at low single-digits in the brick-and-mortar space (provided they are well run, with exceptional vision and planning. Absent these attributes, they could be flat or negative), and double digits in the e-commerce space. The base business in each could be and will be different in most cases, but the future of the two could also be *significantly* different based on growth and opportunity of the individual categories. It's been a challenge to motivate a supplier to look at both segments individually and understand the differences on a category by category basis. Most are significantly behind the market playing catch up due to the way it's changing daily in terms of consumer acquisition of goods and services, and how buyers view each. You should be growing at similar levels or if you are driving change for your own benefit, at higher levels of growth than your customers as a result of taking share from your competitors.

- **How are you supporting each of the two channels in terms of product development?** Brick-and-mortar channels have substantial upfront investments in terms of inventory requirements. Each store must support a certain amount of inventory, which drives significant investment based on the number of locations; whereas the e-commerce channel supports what could be a single source of distribution. In brick-and-mortar, every piece of inventory in every brick and mortar location represents risk if the product doesn't sell or turn appropriately to support the retailer's financial needs. The efficiencies of e-commerce distribution lend themselves to a much larger assortment base that can be developed, tested, and supported due to the lower investment and risk it represents to inventory and the resulting cash flow. If you aren't challenging your team to be more robust in the e-commerce segment in terms of product development, you aren't maximizing your opportunities to drive more assortment placement within your customer base. The risk and cost associated with poorly performing items is significantly more controllable in the e-commerce space than in the brick-and-mortar. Many have gotten the message already and are using the e-commerce channel to test and understand product assortments from a number of different perspectives -- rates of sale, return rates, overall customer interest, and demographic/geographic data, for example -- before investing in brick and mortar inventory. The likelihood that you can put your product on a buyer's website is significantly higher than obtaining space in the brick-and-mortar locations.

- **Is there a vitality goal for product development and if so, is it supported by your customer's ability to keep up with change?** When a supplier has a new product vitality goal -- meaning a percentage of business that is newly created each year and every year going forward -- they control a much more robust piece of the market growth. An important dependency is what kind of growth the market can bear in terms of change, and if it matches the vitality goal of the supplier. For example, often the larger retailers have long lead times to change or add products, primarily due to the planning and set-up phase of moving new items into the stores (another reason why vitality planning should be different for brick-and-mortar vs. e-commerce platforms). If reality dictates 12 months to add a new item to the stores and gauge its success, how often should they change items? If a particular customer can only manage five or less new items a year per category, why would you provide them 10 new items to consider unless they are behind in a segment of the market that is changing rapidly? Many businesses are on a vitality target percentage based on what could be as little as introductions of new items over one year to as much as over five years to help them measure change and its success. It varies by category and customer and it's important for the supplier to understand each customers vitality and how they manage change. Categories can also vary dramatically; for example, technology-driven items change more rapidly than non-technology commodity-based products. The supplier must stay ahead of the curve by bringing new items to the market in a well-planned and timely manner, rather than waiting for the buyer to ask for them. *If the supplier is driving long term innovation through new product development, the supplier improves their leverage in the relationship.*

Question #3: "Is your strategy to push or pull the product through the market?"

How the supplier approaches this particular dynamic is critical in determining how the relationship develops with a buyer, and where the leverage lies as a result. It will also determine both the activity with a customer and the cost of marketing, depending on the approach the supplier decides to take.

Push Strategy: Pushing product through the market is simply defined as a placement strategy. This means the supplier spends most of their time working to gain and grow shelf placement with a buyer, thus defending their position in the market. In the grocery world, the push strategy is significant; many grocers will charge for space in both height and width of the display, while most other retailers in the industry do not. The push strategy lends itself to having 100 choices of BBQ sauce on the shelf, or an entire aisle devoted to cereal, to use two examples. The income shelf placement generates for the profitability for grocers is vital to their survival. In most other retailers' stores, a vendor earns their space through sales and positive productivity, rather than paying for it. Look at a push strategy this way: if I get prominent placement on the shelf, I can win against my competitors based on my value proposition, (price, brand, new product or innovation, etc.). The overall goal in this case is to place your product in front of the customer in the aisle or online via the buyers who own significant foot traffic in their stores to gain share. Push strategies require manpower, extended travel budgets with high expense expectations, and significant relationship-building that must be perpetually maintained. *As you probably surmised, all the leverage in this case lies with the buyer.*

Pull Strategy: The market determines the placement in the pull strategy, meaning the supplier spends most of their time working to gain and grow consumer sentiment and demand for their products via a particular niche, need, or value they have developed that others don't have. Brands like Nike are an excellent example. Can you imagine trying to develop a reputation as an athletic shoe store and not carrying the Nike brand? Or consider the same scenario of trying to gain reputation in your plumbing and bath business. You must carry certain products and brands like Kohler Plumbing and Bath, based on their share of the market and the demand they create. This strategy lends itself to the supplier getting the calls from the buyers asking to sell their products and the supplier determining a significant percentage of how the relationship is structured. Successful pull strategies are extremely difficult to develop and have a high initial cost but offer the most benefit in the long term. Why is the cost "initial" in nature? Once the brand integrity and need in the market are developed, buyer acquisition costs are significantly lower than those investing in a forever ongoing push strategy. Pull strategies must be well defined within the marketing plans and strategies. They also depend on a supplier leading in innovation, while maintaining the market integrity that drives the pull on a continuing basis -- a primary reason why good planning and long-term strategies are significant in driving successful growth and sustainable leverage. Pull strategies require significant marketing budgets; large R&D activity and expense; meaningful consumer research; and fluid, ongoing long-term planning. *As you probably surmised, all the leverage in this case lies with the supplier.*

Question #4: "Do you actually own the leverage you have developed or are you giving it away?" (The defining moments with a buyer, are you working together or against one another?).

The one word every supplier fears is "no." I'm not referring to what the buyer may say; I'm referring to what a supplier <u>*won't say*</u>. What's even more interesting is that the one word every buyer fears from a supplier is also "no," especially when there is no clearly defined reasoning behind it. Every relationship has risks; however, the problem with suppliers - especially those who have no leverage - is that they tend to absorb all the risk. These suppliers are constantly saying yes to a buyer's request, then figuring out the consequences and costs afterward and then embedding them somewhere else in the relationship. The suppliers who own the leverage say no in many cases because their market position doesn't require the action the buyer is asking them to undertake to be successful. Saying yes to any request that doesn't benefit both parties is a defining moment and a shift in leverage between a supplier and buyer. This doesn't mean the supplier *never* says yes; it means forging a collaborative relationship with joint planning to drive benefit and accountability on both sides that doesn't require a yes or a no.

A supplier should *never* give a buyer a yes without getting something in return. The likelihood you will get consistency in obtaining joint benefit is fully dependent on the percentage of leverage the supplier has in the relationship. A supplier's position in the market must be well defined and recognized by the consumer in order to provide leverage in the relationship with a buyer. Everyone in the supplier's organization must be educated to understand the position and know when to say yes and when to say no. Actions in which there is ambiguity in the response (meaning neither yes nor no is appropriate), are opportunities to expand leverage, and if handled correctly, expand it in the supplier's favor. *The goal is for the supplier to provide a substantiated and recognized value to the buyer, which is not available through any other source, thus pushing the leverage in their favor.* Once the leverage is identified, it's critically important to maintain and protect the supplier's position.

Question #5: "Does the supplier understand the goals and long-term financial strategies of their buyers and where they are falling short which creates opportunities?"

Every publicly traded company publishes quarterly and annual results along with forward looking forecasts. Great suppliers are in tune to their customers' quarterly earnings reports, annual reports, and the quarterly calls many companies have with the analysts. Usually quarterly calls are made public through the company's website, including the schedule and instructions for listening in real time or reading past transcripts.

The value lies in understanding what the goals are so you can align them with your selling strategy, then identify where the company may be falling short which creates opportunities. This is a critical activity that every supplier's organization must engage in on a customer-by-customer basis. A retailer's buyer focuses primarily on three areas: sales, inventory productivity, and margins. Any shortfall is usually a direct result of missing a goal in one of these areas.

- **Inventory**: all retailers operate on a simple premise: take cash, buy inventory, sell the inventory for a profit generating more cash, and then repeat. It drives cash flow, which then drives investments and profit for the retailer. The trick for the retailer is to avoid over-investing in inventory or turning the inventory too slowly. In either case, they won't generate enough cash to buy additional inventory when needed. All retailers set turn goals, (how often their total inventory is sold and replenished in a year, the higher the turn rate, the more cash flow that's produced), and the Wall Street analysts pay close attention to the retailers' inventory positions. A slow-down in sales generates swells in inventory, which reduces cash flow; lack of inventory generates gaps in sales because there's not enough product to meet demand. Your goal as a supplier is to understand the buyers' turn plans, the challenges they encounter in meeting those plans, and working with the buyer to help them reach their financial expectations. For a supplier, it goes back to question #1, in being aligned from a distribution and acquisition standpoint with their customers. Just-in-time inventory is critical to the relationship; one of the greatest challenges a buyer faces is to avoid either buying too much inventory or not enough. *If you are helping a buyer reach their inventory goals through improved productivity that increases sales, you are creating leverage in your favor in the relationship.*

- **Sales:** Anytime a buyer isn't making their sales plan, it creates a sense of urgency towards resolving any sales-related issue. Sales is the primary focus; all other projects will fall by the wayside until those related issues are addressed. A supplier can drive leverage by having a joint sales plan that includes accountability on both sides of the equation and drives promotional and new product launch activity, coupled with market growth. Sales should be forecasted and planned through a simple but important formula: *"market growth + new product launches + promotional activity = forecasted sales."*

  - ➢ *Market Growth* defined as what is being driven by the market and overall consumer sentiment, market growth can be positive or negative. Different market segments have different dependencies but, in most cases, this is an external forecast determined by the market, not by any action on the part of the supplier or the buyer. It's the minimum result a supplier should expect, which is the same for all their competitors.

  - ➢ *New Product Launches* should be viewed as <u>incremental</u> growth, where items solve an existing gap in the market, thus creating a new opportunity. The supplier is responsible for ongoing product vitality, while the buyer is responsible for timing and execution. This area provides significant opportunity for improving profitability and increasing share if the appropriate time, energy, and planning is dedicated to it.

  - ➢ *Promotional Activity* generates a price advantage through a new lower cost that is either fueled by new efficiencies from supplier activity that ultimately leads to a new lower price, or bulk buys that the buyer commits to in both quantity and timing to generate foot traffic. Promotional activity has its place but requires year-over-year well planned activity to avoid generating future gaps in the business. For example, if the supplier ran a promotion last year and didn't plan to compensate for it this year, it drives a positive one year and a negative the next, defeating the overall long-term benefits. Promotional activity alone is not a good strategy because it can be never-ending. Think about those retailers, specifically in the department store sector, who are 100% dependent on high-low pricing. If not managed properly and balanced with a good day-to-day pricing strategy, overall positive customer experience, and new product growth, it can result in a never-ending decline in profitability while trying to "prop up" the sales.

All the activity regarding sales must be carefully documented and reviewed on an ongoing basis, preferably every quarter. Planning should be at least three years out, with the first 12 months of detail already agreed upon, including dates, commitments, and accountability. Year two should document the details of agreements under consideration and awaiting approval, and year three should be ideas in progress. To be successful, all three years must have both future and past views. In most cases, new products in conjunction with promotional activity are the keys to generating market share for both the supplier and the buyer. *A supplier who consistently delivers this formula in an accurate and timely manner develops significant leverage in the relationship.*

- **Gross Margin:** All retailers' success depends on the profitability of what they sell. Usually buyers are paid and/or evaluated on the profitability they generate against the financial goals of the company. In many cases, to meet their gross margin growth goals, a buyer looks for a lower cost from a supplier with no path to get there (which, as my first book *The Disappearing Merchant* describes, isn't the best strategy for long-term success). Instead, they should seek, and a supplier should strategically provide a better value proposition with long-term impacts to rising profitability. Translated, this means:

- ➢ Products with new innovations drive better value for the consumer and should drive better margins for you and the buyer. Any new product introduced ahead of the market should provide a higher average ticket and higher margins. If not, the strategy hasn't been well thought out. If a buyer asks for a lower cost on a new product, this is a prime place to say "no," as it's a poor strategy on both the buyer's and the supplier's part to intentionally drive down financial opportunity at the onset of a new introduction. A much more successful strategy in the long run is to reduce the price in the future to drive value as the market changes and becomes more competitive, rather than increase the price to drive margin -- and alienate consumer sentiment in the process.

- ➢ Driving jointly planned and executed efficiencies that reduce operational costs for both parties can play a significant role in the relationship. Although the practice of identifying where efficiencies can be improved is critical to success, in most cases, it rarely receives the appropriate time and planning to support the opportunities. The primary reason? The buyer will take all the reduced costs associated with the results for themselves, which results in suppliers not participating or generating the projects to start with. A supplier must understand and recognize the efficiency opportunities they can impact, including but not limited to shelf management; marketing; transportation and supply chain; promotional scheduling; and operational efficiencies on the website or in the brick and mortar locations. Once identified, these opportunities must be leveraged in the ongoing battle for cost. When a supplier recognizes and brings them to the attention of the buyer, the work associated with the task adds significant value to the relationship. There is a point of contention where "no" is appropriate when a buyer has the expectation of not sharing in the efficiencies and taking all of the reduced cost being created by the supplier. It must be clear that this is a shared path to operational improvement, and *not* a singular one in which the supplier absorbs the cost while the buyer enjoys the benefit.

Filling in the gaps where opportunities exist for the buyer to improve their business significantly improves the suppliers leverage in the relationship.

CHAPTER 3

MANAGING THE ULTIMATE "BAD GUY" BUYER

In every supplier's portfolio of customers, there is normally the presence of what I term "bad guy" buyers. "Bad guy" buyers exhibit many negative traits such as little- to- no integrity, borderline dishonesty, an inability to keep commitments, and a tendency to leverage the suppliers 100% of the time for their own self-benefit. These are the most difficult and frustrating relationships to manage, especially when the supplier's business relies on the buyer for a large portion of their success. The "bad guy" buyer knows it and uses it to build leverage for themselves. You can term this a number of different ways, but I view it as a buyer with a "King Kong" attitude who employs the negotiation strategy of "do it or else." You can manage this situation in a multitude of ways, all of them requiring significant effort:

1). **Take the time to develop and consistently communicate your position regarding the success you are providing for the buyer's business. Set the stage for what is at stake by** carefully outlining and documenting the supplier's leverage, along with the financial benefits each one represents for the buyer. Clear and factual communication without emotion is important to maintaining your integrity in the relationship. The goal here is not to put the buyer on the defensive, but to educate them on an ongoing basis with constant, meaningful updates. One of the most difficult situations I dealt with as a merchant was controlling the emotions that come with negotiating a frustrating situation. (Those who know me are now laughing uncontrollably that I am pitching vendor discussions without emotion. I admit, it's a learning that occurred late in my career that I wish I'd mastered much earlier!). The more you educate the buyer without emotion, the more the buyer understands your importance to their success. The activity should result in a better long-term position for the supplier in the relationship.

2). **Document and confirm in detail all conversations with the buyer/merchant with something as simple as an email after a call or a meeting.** If you've both made decisions that impact your business and rely on an action to which the buyer has committed, documentation protects the supplier's position when they make the necessary investments to execute the buyer's requested action. This could involve building additional existing product inventory or launching new products. Here's an example of a simple email communication/dialogue:

"Thank you for your time and commitment to our business at today's meeting. We'll begin the process of building the additional inventory of (XXXXX units), to ship on (date), to support the promotional activity you will be advertising during the following quarter. We will follow up on the success as the promotion is executed and appreciate your business."

It's important to communicate immediately following your conversations to maintain integrity in the actions discussed.

Keep in mind, an email will document the agreed upon commitments without imposing a directive to "sign this" -- a practice that alienates most buyers, especially a "bad buyer." In most organizations, even if the sender receives no response to a follow-up email, it's considered a commitment by the recipient unless they respond in writing to deny the validity of the content. This type of communication is not intended to be a legal move; it's only intended purpose is to document the relationship and the commitments you have made. On a subconscious level, it also puts the buyer on notice that the supplier is tracking the actions of both parties in the relationship for future follow-up. As an executive who was responsible for a multitude of merchants and suppliers, it's amazing how many situations I encountered where a supplier called to request I intervene in a commitment that had not yet been executed. My first action was always to ask for documentation regarding the project and the communication between the supplier and the buyer. More often than not, there was none. A supplier simply cannot allow themselves to be put in this situation, *ever.*

3) **Know when it's time to get others in the buyer's organization involved in a problem.** As a supplier, when you do business with a buyer/merchant and they explicitly ask you not to contact anyone other than themselves within their organization, (especially if there is a non-implied or implied threat to the supplier that doing so could drive punitive actions), it's a glaring warning sign you must take seriously.

What are the primary reasons a buyer engages in this type of action?

A. They lack confidence in their own decisions
B. They are intentionally hiding circumstances they don't want others to have knowledge of
C. They are positioning themselves to do what they want, when they want, and without consequence.

There are <u>no</u> reasonable reasons for a buyer to take this position in any situation.

Regardless of the reason, when this scenario arises, it's time for the supplier to contact the person to whom the buyer reports. Most suppliers won't take this action out of fear of reprisal, but the cost of inaction comes with major long-term ramifications the supplier may not be able to control or reverse. The supplier must act to minimize any "he said, she said" activity. Translated, this means a supplier must have the documentation available as an outline for the discussion with the buyer's leader. I would even suggest including the buyer on the call or in the meeting, giving them up-front notice about the action you're taking, and an overview of the meeting outline provided. This isn't a "covert" activity; it's an above-board discussion about unfulfilled commitments by the buyer and the organization. As a consultant, suppliers have actually solicited my help in "getting a buyer fired" to solve their issues. I refuse to participate in these situations because in most cases, the supplier has failed to protect their end of the conversation, or to do the necessary work to gain appropriate leverage in the relationship. Often, a long look in the mirror will reveal a number of shortfalls on the supplier's side. Ultimately you have to ask yourself, "What's the plan if a 'bad guy' buyer gets replaced with another 'bad guy' buyer?"

4) **Build relationships at all levels of the buyer's organization.** This goes a long way in securing the stability and consistency of the activity between a supplier and a buyer if others in the buyer's organization understand the commitments and results being obtained. It's especially helpful if a particular buyer's position turns over on a regular basis and the supplier finds themselves routinely starting over in the relationship. In the industry this is usually termed as "new butts in the seat". Unfortunately, the larger the supplier is to the retailer, the easier this is to accomplish due to the size of the risk. However,

regardless of size, there are a number of helpful behaviors the supplier can engage in:

- **Attend the retailer's community and charitable events.** Regardless of the size of their organization, in almost every case, a retailer makes a commitment to their community or a charitable organization, (often more than one). They typically depend on their associates and the supplier base for donations and participation in these events to maximize the positive impacts they can provide for the needs of the community. It's important for suppliers to budget and participate in these activities because all levels of management attend many of these events and, they are usually accessible. These occasions often present opportunities for the supplier, based on their participation and donation to the cause. The further up the ladder in terms of size of the commitment, the further up the ladder the relationship between the supplier and retailer can develop. It's up to the supplier to determine the level of support they want to provide, keeping in mind it is most often a tax-deductible expense that could go a long way toward building a mutually beneficial relationship.

- **When invited, suppliers should attend the retailer's business meetings, regardless of the topic or the accessibility to management.** Many suppliers receive invitations to attend learning sessions, annual marketing meetings, supply chain conferences, etc. attended by the total retail organization or, at a minimum, its key leaders. These events present another opportunity to learn more about how to engage in the business and meet and develop relationships with others at different levels of the organization.

- **It's not a good strategy to invite leaders in the retail organization to scheduled meetings with the buyer to discuss ongoing business.** Yes, you want to develop relationships with them, but this is not the time or the place. In most successful retail organizations, leadership expects the buyer to run the day-to-day business without their intervention; they do not want to be leveraged to make decisions that fall under a buyer's jurisdiction. Meeting the leadership in other types of casual settings offers the most benefit unless you are dealing with a serious issue. Remember, it's just as uncomfortable for a buyer to conduct a meeting in front of their leadership as it is for a supplier in front of their own.

The "bad guy" buyer doesn't have to own the leverage in the relationship. Taking specific steps to mitigate their negative behaviors improves the leverage position of the supplier.

CHAPTER 4

UNDERSTANDING AND MANAGING A SUPPLIER'S SELF WORTH

I cannot overstate the importance of a supplier understanding their own self-worth to improve their leverage. When a supplier can't articulate the dependency they have created resulting in success in the market, they can't develop leverage in any of their relationships. It boils down to one singular question we mentioned earlier: ***"What does your company provide to a buyer that can't be duplicated anywhere else?*** Consider Amazon: how many innovations across all aspects of their business have they introduced and continue to introduce that may be duplicated over time by competitors, yet it seems everyone else is always playing catch-up? How does a supplier compete with that kind of activity?

Did you ever play this game in high school after you obtained your driver's license? You drive up to a friend's house to pick them up. You honk, you wait until they walk out to the car and reach for the door handle, but before they can grab it, you drive forward about 10 feet, laugh hysterically, and then repeat...well, that's the game Amazon plays with their competitors day in and day out. Just when you think you have caught up, they drive away again. Amazon keeps tabs on all their competitors *via the rearview mirror.* My take: if you can duplicate a similar strategy and view your competitors in the rear view mirror on a consistent basis, then you must understand you can **never** let your competitor get in the car with you, much less give them access to the steering wheel. You will never get them out. You must consistently develop leverage others aren't providing in the market...not just now, ***but forever.***

The key is to take the information gathered and formulate an easy-to-understand business strategy that has the accountability and buy-in of the organization. The organization must own the long-term health and execution of the strategy. It's a fairly simple formula that can be manipulated in a number of ways, but its foundation is fundamental:

1). The executive team collects feedback from the associates; studies the market past, present, and future; and talks extensively to the end-users and the existing customer base.

2). The results collected and the opportunistic market gaps identified are formulated into specific strategies that the company has the width and breadth to execute. (Don't fold in "pie in the sky activity" that the company will never achieve; over time it will create frustration in the organization, not to mention it's a waste of resources.)

3). Give specific leaders in the organization the responsibility to build a strategic plan around timing and cost to execute the strategy.

4). The executive team sets up an approval process, leads the team in the detailed development, and decides on the toll gates and timing for check-in to execute the strategies that have been developed.

5). This is always a three-year view: year one is in progress with dates and expected results monitored for execution and return on the activity; year two identifies all activity but waits on approval and timing; year three involves the approval by the executive team on all requested activity before details and timing are determined (sound familiar?).

6). On a quarterly basis, monitor and update the activity and hold the leaders of the specific strategies accountable for the timing, execution, and results.

All the activity has flexibility and can be managed/designed in a number of ways. The important outcome is the determination of what a company has accomplished, is going to accomplish, and is working towards in the future which becomes the "self-worth." The dynamics of creating a competitive advantage that no one else has yet to attain is the dependency that should be articulated to prospective and current buyers. If a supplier can reach this level of consistent strategy development and execution, their leverage position in the market will dramatically change...always for the better.

Examples of "self-worth" statements:

- **"We have the lowest cost in the market."**

  (Difficult to maintain over time unless the supplier's volume continues to grow while their competitor's volume does not. If a buyer can obtain the lowest cost, at a minimum it grows their margin or lowers their retails, but it is rarely sustainable and becomes a competitive threat in the future).

- **"We have the latest innovation important to the consumer that no one else has."**

(This is the most attractive self-worth statement as long as others do not copy it quickly, especially at a lower cost. The supplier must consistently deliver new innovation going forward. It's not just about new products; it's about new product that drives incremental business. The primary reason? You measure product vitality by % of your sales in new products, not the number of items introduced. This is the most defensible and profitable position to be in with a buyer. Every buyer wants to be known for being first to market with new products and reap the benefits of the results that driving sustainable market share provides).

- **"We have just-in-time inventory we can deliver to multiple destinations, including direct- to-home, which comes with no additional cost to the buyer."**

(Attractive to the buyer because it results in improved turns and cash flow maximizing their inventory investments with low risk).

- **"We own the Top 3 Consumer Report-rated items for our category in the market".**

(Attractive to the buyer as it drives quality with low returns, improving customer satisfaction).

- **"We guarantee a 99% fill rate on all shipments on an annualized basis".**

(Attractive to a buyer since it maximizes sales by improving in-stock rates).

Depending on the market and categories they support, there are a host of other self-worth statements a supplier can adopt, but these are excellent examples that will command the attention of a buyer.

Keep in mind, self-worth isn't exclusively determined by a single competitive advantage. Exceptionally strong organizations are leveraged to their benefit in a number of different areas of the market. Imagine how strong your position is if all 5 examples above fall under the umbrella of a single supplier? The amount of control you have in driving long-term profitability and growth would be self-dependent, not dependent on the decisions made by a buyer or others to whom you sell in the market.

CHAPTER 5

DEVELOPING THE ELEVATOR SPEECH

How, when, and what message a supplier communicates on a consistent basis determines the integrity and validity of their "self-worth."

If you asked an hourly associate, a manager, a director, and an executive from a specific supplier the same question, "Tell me what your company's competitive advantage is in today's market?", what would they say if they only had 30 seconds to articulate their company's self-worth? What if each answer was different? What if each answer was the same? If the answers are different, it creates the impression that associates at different levels of the organization have varying understandings of what the company delivers. Some may be real; some may be fabricated.

The second answer delivers an entirely different message in that the company is focused on the deliverables that drive success as seen by their customers. If everyone in the organization is talking and living the same deliverables and supporting a consistent goal, the message becomes quite clear to the buying community on whom they should depend on for success.

In every business I managed over my career, we discussed at length what our elevator speech was and why it was important. It helped everyone at every level to stay focused on what was vitally important to growth and success. It also provided a consistent message for those outside of the organization to know what was being delivered in terms of market value. Think about it this way, if a buyer asks "Why should I do business with you instead of anyone else?", and after listening to your response, replies he already has that success, then you and your organization must realize you have the wrong message. On the other hand, if the buyer responds with "I have to have that," you know your message is on-point. Leverage will turn in your favor and will be yours to own, manage, and grow for the future.

CHAPTER 6

IS THIS REALLY POSSIBLE OR JUST PIE IN THE SKY?

Everything I've discussed isn't fabricated or a pipe dream; it's the reality of what I have experienced over my career. In my efforts to achieve success, I took all the hazardous shortcuts, leveraging every "bad guy" buyer behavior one could exhibit -- sometimes all of them at once. (As I laid out in my first book, **The Disappearing Merchant,** there are 10 sins a buyer must not commit. Unfortunately, at some point in my career I was really good at all of them). I stood on the table and screamed and pounded my fist; threatened suppliers; took away business; and found myself in a number of situations where I was leveraged and didn't much like it. One supplier or another would find a way around it, and I was constantly looking out the front windshield at my competitor trying to catch up rather than watching them in the rear-view mirror, yeah...not much fun. I didn't like it and felt incredibly frustrated day in and day out. It wasn't until I listened intently to my mentors, leaders, *the suppliers who had a great message and did the hard work*, my peers, and those around me working in other functional areas that I realized I had the wrong understanding of my real goals and responsibilities. This book describes what reality is and can be for many suppliers, if they will *just put in the work required to get there.*

Late in my career, I had the pleasure of experiencing true partnership with a number of suppliers. What it took was listening, and listening, and listening, and listening again, to their goals, challenges, and intentions, and how they were positioned in the market. Once I had a solid understanding of how I could help them achieve their goals and success, I aligned them with my own instead of manipulating them to my advantage or demanding something different.

Different suppliers owned different pieces of the market and with time, skill, and hard work, it developed into a very successful portfolio for the businesses under my management. That initial conversation always helped to set up the relationship so I could help guide and teach, rather than scold and ridicule. In the end, I developed cooperative business relationships and the results we experienced together reflected the long-term goals and strategies we both assumed accountability for, lived by, and succeeded by. They delivered mutual success in all the areas we targeted. I no longer had the need to have "line reviews" or "auction business" because we always had a mutual plan on how to improve the business year in and year out, not just for now, but perpetually *for everyone involved.* The game was no longer who can take what from whom, or who wins the ultimate tug of war for leverage; it was about throwing away the rope for the mutual benefit and success of both parties.

The dream for this industry is that both the supplier and the merchant realize the long-term roles they must play in the market for the mutual benefit of the consumer. Should that become the case, and merchants throw out the behaviors associated with the 10 sins of a buyer, while suppliers put time, energy, and work into determining their self-worth and how to deliver it to the market, we can reach the maximum consumer value we do not see today, at least not in a consistent and well-planned manner.

I would much rather be looking in the rear-view mirror and enjoying what I see rather than being face-forward, nose to the windshield, and my foot on the accelerator, trying to play catch up...so should you.

WHAT'S YOUR LEVERAGE SCORE?

On a scale of 1 to 120, how is your supplier organization doing in terms of leveraging your self-worth in the market? Take this quick test to find out by circling the answer that best fits your organization and adding up your total results.

1). I can consistently get the buyer/merchant with whom I already do business with on the phone and commit and keep a meeting without having to expend a significant amount of effort and follow-up.

A.   All the time, regardless of the topic. (10 points)
B.   Half the time, depending on the topic and whether it includes a round of golf. (5 points)
C.   Never without repeated begging and calling everyone I know in the organization, regardless of the topic or what I offer up. (0 points)

2). I can consistently get a reasonable introduction either by phone or in person with a prospective buyer.

A.   Majority of the time, regardless of the company and who I know. (10 points)
B.   Half the time, depending on the company and who I know. (5 points)
C.   Never without begging, stalking, offering to take the buyer to dinner, or sending gifts regardless of the company. (0 points)

3). We plan for the what is and the what if's consistently and for the long term with a great degree of success.

A.   We review once a quarter and have a running 3-year plan/strategy that everyone understands and produces results. (10 points)

B.   We review once a year and plan each year primarily around the *what is* with some discussion on the *what ifs.* (5 points)

C.   Don't have any idea what you are talking about. (0 points)

4). Our product distribution and transportation strategies line up with our individual customers and provides a benefit to both parties in managing cost long term.

A.   With every individual customer, we are aligned long term as a strategic partner in their distribution needs. (10 points)

B.   We are only aligned long term with our largest customer as a strategy partner in their distribution needs. (5 points)

C.   We don't have a distribution strategy; we just ship the product wherever we are told. (0 points)

5). Do you have a separate and well-defined long-term product development strategy between the brick-and-mortar and e-commerce businesses?

A.   We maintain two different product development strategies between the two businesses, each with its own dedicated staff and business goals. (10 points)

B.   We maintain a single product development strategy with an emphasis on e-commerce as the testing channel to eventually feed the brick-and-mortar channels with a single staff. (5 points)

C.   Our product strategy is to copy what everyone else does (with minor changes to avoid patent issues) and manufacture outside of the U.S. to cut costs. (0 points).

6). Do you have a product vitality goal as a percent of your business that is commensurate with the market growth and changes buyers regularly make?

A. Yes, it's a one-to-three-year goal that is a percentage of our business based on the category and market. It's monitored, reviewed, changed as needed at least on an annualized basis. It can vary by customer, depending on the competitive position and their ability to change in a fast-paced environment. (10 points)

B. Yes, it's one goal for the total company we review once a year or so. (5 points)

C. I don't understand what vitality means or how to treat it if I get it. (0 points)

7). Do you have an executed and defined "push" strategy or "pull" strategy?

A. We have a pull strategy that is successful in the market in driving placement due to unsolicited buyers request. (10 points)

B. We have a pull strategy that is working with some, but not with others. It needs refining and better development to support the future. We still rely on a push strategy for a large percentage of our business. (5 points)

C. I thought we got rid of the rope? (0 points)

8). Does your organization have a strategy that will maintain the leverage in the relationship once it's developed?

A. There is great understanding in our company on where we give and take in the relationship with each individual customer. We say no when it's appropriate and get benefit in return when we say yes. (10 points)

B.   We only say yes when the request is discussed and approved internally with all levels of our organization. We rarely say no, due to the risk it places on the relationship in terms of lost business.

C.   We just say "maybe" and then hope the question or request just goes away over time. (0 points)

9). Are you tracking the quarterly public results of your customer base, then adjusting to the changes in the market?

A.   We expect our team to be in tune with the strategies and results of each customer by paying attention to the public information provided via all channels. We meet regularly to understand how to help with the challenges and make sure we are participating in the successes at a minimum on a bi-annual basis. (10 points)

B.   As a company, we have a single person who keeps track of our largest customers and reports back to the team any significant announcement that may impact our business. (5 points)

C.   We don't have a good internet connection and really don't know where to find this information. This doesn't really impact us anyway. (0 points)

10). We regularly discuss the difficult buyers in our portfolio that we need to manage and work towards developing a meaningful, non-confrontational relationship.

A.   We pay particular attention to the tough buyers, keep excellent documentation, and develop relationships around them with other leaders and influencers in the buyer's organization to help maintain consistency and balance in the relationship. (10 points)

B.   We know who they are and have them identified but expect our sales team to make do with the situation and keep them happy to protect our business. (5 points)

C.   We just say yes to whatever they ask for, then take them for a golf outing once a month and make sure they always win. (0 points)

11). Do you have a strong self-worth statement that both those inside and outside of your organization validate and promote?

A.   Every member of our organization understands the self-worth value we have created, and can articulate it, along with our customers who can validate the success it creates. (10 points)

B.   The executive team drives the company's self-worth where appropriate and shares it with those who they feel should understand it. (5 points)

C.   Not sure what we stand for or what our customers actually believe is the value we provide for their business. (0 points)

12). Do all members of your organization articulate the company's worth, long-term value, and overall goals in an elevator speech that is consistent at all levels?

A.   No matter what level of the organization you speak to or when, you get the same articulated value proposition our organization delivers to the market on a consistent basis. (10 points)

B.   The executive team knows what we are delivering and why. (5 points)

C.   Don't ask me; I have no idea. (0 points)

Understanding the results:

90-120 points: You are in a favorable position and own a good portion of your destination and success.

40 to 90 points: There is opportunity...and much more work to do to create real self-worth.

0-40 points: You shut the doors yesterday; you just don't know it yet.

ABOUT THE AUTHOR

Mike Hogenmiller is a 40+ year veteran of the retail home improvement industry. His experience includes both operations and merchandising where he assumed responsibility for businesses as large as $6 billion+. Mike's background encompasses wholesale and retail associated with brick-and-mortar as well as e-commerce channels. His individual merchant responsibilities had an annualized volume from as small as $100,000 to as much as $400 million with a single supplier giving him experience in managing complex businesses with large and small manufacturers both domestic and international. Mike served as a mentor to leaders inside and outside the industry through organizations such as American Corporate Partners. Green Belt Certified in Six Sigma, he was a teacher and trainer in dedicated programs developed by several of the companies he worked for. Although he retired from the industry in 2016, Mike continues to work as an industry consultant for a number of domestic and international businesses including manufacturing, retail, and service providers. He resides in Atlanta Georgia with his wife of 42 years, where they are very much enjoying retirement, travel, and spending time with family.

NOTES

www.ingramcontent.com/pod-product-compliance
Lightning Source LLC
Chambersburg PA
CBHW031544060726
47590CB00004BA/1505